Usborne
THE BIG
BUG
SEARCH

Caroline Young

Illustrated by Ian Jackson

Designed by Andy Dixon

Edited by Kamini Khanduri

Contents

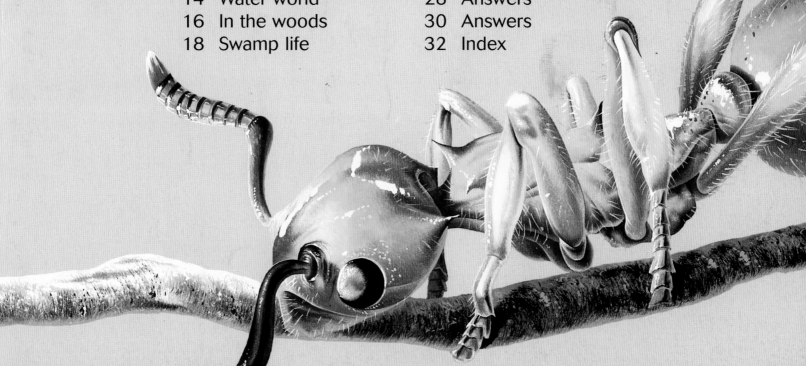

About this book

This is a puzzle book all about bugs. If you look hard, you'll find beetles, butterflies, spiders, snails, slugs and hundreds of other creepy-crawlies from all around the world. This is how the puzzles work.

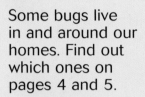

Some bugs live in and around our homes. Find out which ones on pages 4 and 5.

See inside these trapdoor spiders' burrows in the scorching desert on pages 6 and 7.

This cockroach from Madagascar makes a strange noise. Find out what it is on pages 8 and 9.

There are about 100 bugs in each big picture. In real life, there wouldn't be as many in one place at the same time.

Around the outside of each big picture, there are lots of little pictures.

The writing next to each little picture tells you how many of that bug to look for in the big picture.

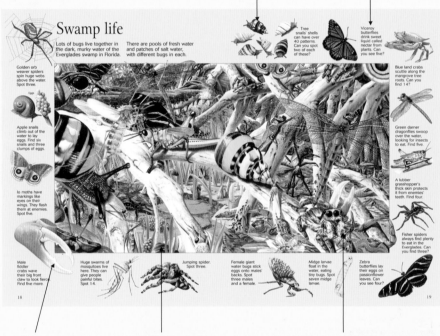

This crab coming out of the big picture counts as a little picture too.

This part of a snail's shell counts as one snail.

A spider is about to eat this mosquito, but the mosquito still counts.

Some of the bugs are very easy to spot, but some are tiny, or hidden against their background. If you get really stuck, you'll find all the answers on pages 28–31.

On pages 10 and 11, you can find out why you should steer clear of these wandering spiders from Peru.

These pretty emperor gum moths live among the eucalyptus trees in Australia. See what else does on pages 12 and 13.

2

Worker bees have busy lives. Find out about the jobs they do in a beehive on page 25.

Queen termites are much bigger than any other termites. On page 24, you can see a queen inside her home.

Hidden extras

You'll find one of these animals hiding somewhere on each page. On pages split into two halves (pages 8–9, 20–21 and 24–25), there's one animal in each half.

In South Africa, a gang of assassin bugs can be very dangerous. You'll discover why on pages 22 and 23.

Aardvark

Orang-utan

Mouse

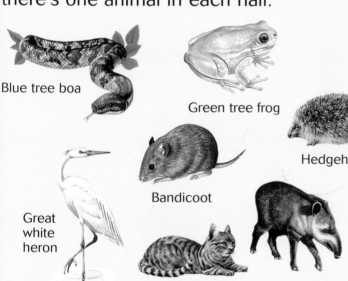

Blue tree boa

Green tree frog

Kudu

Ring-tailed lemur

Hedgehog

Bandicoot

Great white heron

Cat

Tapir

Alligator

Burrowing owl

Hairy bird-eating spiders live deep in the jungle. Find out more about them on pages 20 and 21.

Young bugs

Young bugs are often called nymphs or larvae. They may look very different from their parents. Here's how a dragonfly grows up.

Adult flying

Dragonflies lay eggs in or near water. Each egg hatches into a dragonfly nymph.

Nymph

As it grows, the nymph loses its skin. The last time it does this, it becomes an adult.

Adult emerging

Lubber grasshoppers live in the Everglades swamp in the USA. You'll find them on pages 18 and 19.

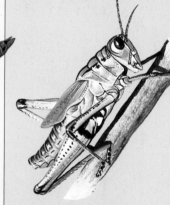

Pond snails make life easier for all the animals living in a pond. Find out how on pages 14 and 15.

Woods are home to hundreds of different minibeasts. You can see some of them on pages 16 and 17.

Homes and gardens

Not all minibeasts live in wild places. Many live in gardens, parks, and even in and around houses. This is a picture of a house in Britain. Can you spot 158 creatures here?

Snails leave sticky trails which show where they have been. Can you track down ten?

Most fleas drink the blood of animals. Some also drink human blood. Spot ten.

Female garden spiders are bigger than males and often eat them after mating. Spot eight spiders.

Houseflies' mouths are like a mop, soaking up liquid food. Find ten houseflies.

Cinnabar moth

Unlike most moths, cinnabar moths fly by day. Spot seven moths and six caterpillars.

Caterpillar

Lacewings sleep somewhere warm all winter. They turn brown while they sleep. Find 14.

Cockroaches have flat bodies. They can squeeze under things to hide. Spot 11.

4

Male

Female common blue butterfly

Only male common blue butterflies are really blue. Spot four of each sex.

Honeybees carry yellow pollen from flowers in "baskets" on their back legs. Can you find ten?

Zebra spiders creep up behind their victims and pounce on them. Find five.

Their name means "100 feet" but no centipedes have that many. Can you spot six?

Wasps like anything sweet, including our food. They'll sting you if you annoy them. Spot 13.

Devil's coach-horses arch their bodies to scare off enemies. Spot six coach-horses.

Earwigs lift their fierce-looking tails if they are scared, but they can't hurt you. Spot nine.

Tail

Greenflies suck the juice out of plants for their food. Can you spot 17?

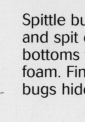

Spittle bugs blow air and spit out of their bottoms to make foam. Find eight bugs hidden in foam.

5

Cactus city

This dry desert in the north of Mexico doesn't look like a very comfortable home, but thousands of bugs live here. Many stay in cool underground burrows during the hot day.

Some people keep Mexican red-kneed bird-eating spiders as pets. Can you find four here?

Painted grasshoppers are named after their bright-looking bodies. Can you spot ten?

Harvester ants collect seeds and store them deep underground. Find 15 busy ants.

Hercules beetles are some of the biggest insects in the world. Can you spot six?

Whip scorpions have a long, thin tail like a whip. It can't hurt you, though. Spot five.

Ant-lion larvae dig pits in the sand. When other bugs fall in, they eat them. Find three.

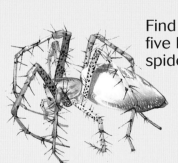

Find five lynx spiders.

Tarantula hawk wasps lay their eggs on tarantula spiders' bodies. Can you find seven of them?

When insects pass a trapdoor spider's home, it flips up its "door" and grabs them. Spot four.

Scorpions lurk in cool burrows until the sun sets. Then they go hunting. Spot six.

Giant red velvet mites hatch out after rain and rush around looking for food. Spot ten.

Some honey ants hang upside down in the nest. Their tummies are full of honey. Spot 13.

Blister beetles sting your skin if you touch them. Find four blister beetles.

Yucca moths only lay their eggs in a yucca plant's flowers. Spot five yucca moths.

Tarantula. Find six.

A southern black widow spider will only bite you if you annoy it. Can you spot four?

Island paradise

The island of Madagascar is home to many bugs that aren't found anywhere else. The bugs on this page live in thick, dry woods. Those on the opposite page live in a rainforest.

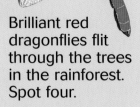

Brilliant red dragonflies flit through the trees in the rainforest. Spot four.

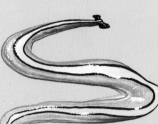

Striped flatworms slither across the forest floor after it has rained. Can you find four?

Weevils often have long noses, but giraffe-necked weevils have long necks. Find four.

Huge emperor dragonflies catch insects flying past. Can you spot six of them?

Some stick insects grow fake "moss" on their bodies as a disguise. Find three.

Thorn spiders look like prickly jewels in their huge webs. Find four.

Giant millipedes can be poisonous, so few animals eat them. Can you find five?

This praying mantis nymph is very well disguised. Can you spot four?

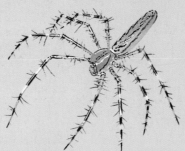

Green lynx spiders blend in with their leafy surroundings. Find four.

Pill millipedes can't run from enemies. They roll into a ball instead. Spot six.

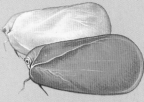

Rosea bugs look a little like leaves. If a bird pecks one, the whole group flies off. Find 27.

Hairy weevils only live in Madagascar. Spot seven of each of these.

Longhorn beetles lay their eggs in dead wood. Later, their larvae eat it. Find seven.

Hissing cockroaches hiss by blowing air out of two holes in their tummies. Find five.

Can you find four shield bug adults and four nymphs?

Adult

Nymph

Spot six butterflies with their wings open and five with their wings shut.

Dazzling display

Some of the most beautiful insects in the world live in rainforests, but they are often hard to spot. Can you find 95 minibeasts in this rainforest in Peru, in South America?

Find nine leaf beetles.

A wandering spider's bite is so poisonous it can kill a person. Can you find two?

Thornbugs look like thorns. Their disguise fools hungry birds. Spot ten.

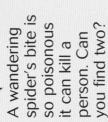

When Hamadryas butterflies fly, their wings make clicking noises. Can you spot four?

Some assassin bugs have spiky bodies. Enemies find them hard to chew. Can you find seven?

Hawk moth caterpillars look pretty but taste nasty, so birds leave them alone. Spot five.

Many gorgeous grasshoppers live in these forests. Find three of each of these kinds.

Long-legged stilt bugs have long, skinny legs that look a little like stilts. Find five.

These bright bugs must taste good because local people eat them. Find six.

Male harlequin beetles guard females with their long front legs. Find seven harlequin beetles.

Female

Male

This grasshopper hides by staying still and hoping it looks like a stick. Spot three.

Bark bugs are hard to spot. They blend into the background. Find seven.

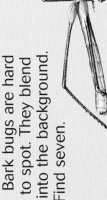

Morpho butterfly. Spot four.

Male Hercules beetles use their horns to push other males away. Spot four.

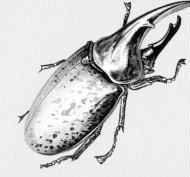

Leafcutter ants eat fungus. They help it grow by covering it with chewed leaves. Find 16.

Between the trees

All kinds of amazing bugs live in the thick eucalyptus forests of eastern Australia. Ants as big as your toes go marching past, and poisonous spiders lurk in dark corners.

Emperor gum moths only lay their eggs on eucalyptus trees. Find three.

Sawfly larvae wave their heads and spit bitter liquid at their enemies. Find nine.

Female redback spiders are much more poisonous than males. Can you spot three?

Processionary moth caterpillars leave a long silk thread behind them. Find 11.

Fierce Sydney funnel-web spiders only live near the city of Sydney. Spot four.

Bulldog ants are the biggest, fiercest ants in the world. Can you spot 12 of them?

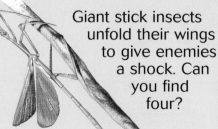

Giant stick insects unfold their wings to give enemies a shock. Can you find four?

Net throwing spiders throw a net of silk over their victims. Spot two more.

Some crickets flash their bright backs at enemies to scare them. Find five.

Bogong moths can eat whole fields of grain if they get together. Spot four.

Common grass yellow butterflies sip water from puddles in hot weather. Spot 23.

Emperor gum moth caterpillars have bright spikes to warn enemies off. Find four.

Gliding spiders can stretch out two flaps of skin and glide through the air. Find four.

Some people dig moth caterpillars called "witchetty grubs" out of tree trunks and eat them. Find six.

There are over 450 different types of shield bugs in Australia. Can you spot nine of this kind?

Monarch butterflies can fly up to 130km (80 miles) in one day. Find five.

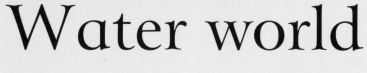

Water world

Ponds are perfect homes for many small creatures. They are often nurseries for young insects too. Can you spot 121 minibeasts in this North American pond?

Fisher spiders crawl down plants, catch fish, then haul them up to eat. Spot eight.

Tube

Mosquito larvae dangle under the surface of ponds. They breathe through a tube. Spot seven.

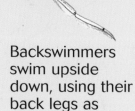

Backswimmers swim upside down, using their back legs as oars. Find six.

Stoneflies can't fly well, so they sit beside the water most of the time. Spot nine.

Damselflies can't walk well. They use their legs to grab hold of plants. Spot seven.

Water striders skim lightly across the surface of the pond. Spot eight water striders.

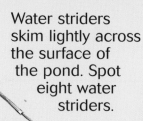

Fishermen put fake caddisflies on their hooks to attract fish. Spot six real caddisflies.

Pond snails do a very useful job. They eat plants and make the water much clearer. Find 11.

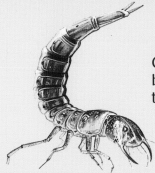

Great diving beetle larvae bite their victims and then suck out their insides. Find five.

Water scorpions lurk just below the surface, grabbing passing insects. Spot six.

Dragonfly nymphs have jaws that shoot out to crunch up food. Can you spot five?

Caddisfly larvae are safe inside a case covered with pebbles and shells. Find five.

Whirligig beetles can look into the air and under the water at the same time. Find 15.

Great diving beetles have strong back legs to help them swim and dive. Spot ten.

Water stick insects breathe air through a narrow breathing tube. Find five stick insects.

Adult mayflies never eat. They just mate, lay eggs and die. Find nine.

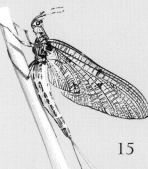

In the woods

If you walked through this wood in northern France, thousands of eyes might be watching you. Tiny creatures make their homes up in the trees, or down on the ground.

Male stag beetles fight with their sharp antlers, but rarely hurt each other. Find six.

Wood ants squirt acid out of their bottoms to attack enemies. Can you spot 20?

Crane flies have six legs. They can survive losing one or two of them. Find eight.

Hedge snails are easy for birds to spot, so they try to stay hidden. Find six snails.

Darter dragonflies flit through the trees in woodland clearings. Can you spot three?

Male empid flies give females a bug wrapped in silk while they mate. Find 12.

Bumblebees fly from flower to flower, collecting pollen. Spot four bumblebees.

Antenna

Longhorn beetles don't have horns, just antennae that look like them. Can you spot seven?

Burying beetles lay their eggs next to a dead animal. When the eggs hatch into larvae, they eat it. Spot ten.

Hornets chew bark to make a soggy mixture. They use it to build nests. Find four.

The amount of purple you can see on a purple emperor butterfly's wings depends on the light. Spot six.

Bark beetles lay their eggs in tree bark. When the eggs hatch, the larvae eat the bark. Find 11.

Large black slugs slither along the woodland floor, leaving a slimy trail. Spot seven.

Poplar hawk moths can see in the dark, so they fly at night. Find five.

Male horseflies drink plant juices but females need to drink animals' blood. Spot four.

Crab spiders lie in wait for insects in flowers. Then they attack and kill them. Spot three.

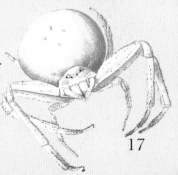

17

Swamp life

Lots of bugs live together in the dark, murky water of the Everglades swamp in Florida.

There are pools of fresh water and patches of salt water, with different bugs in each.

Golden orb weaver spiders spin huge webs above the water. Spot three.

Eggs

Apple snails climb out of the water to lay eggs. Find six snails and three clumps of eggs.

Io moths have markings like eyes on their wings. They flash them at enemies. Spot five.

Male fiddler crabs wave their big front claw to look fierce. Find five more.

Huge swarms of mosquitoes live here. They can give people painful bites. Spot 14.

Jumping spider. Spot three.

18

Tree snails' shells can have over 40 patterns. Can you spot two of each of these?

Viceroy butterflies drink sweet liquid called nectar from plants. Can you see five?

Blue land crabs scuttle along the mangrove tree roots. Can you find 14?

Green darner dragonflies swoop over the water, looking for insects to eat. Find five.

A lubber grasshopper's thick skin protects it from enemies' teeth. Find four.

Fisher spiders always find plenty to eat in the Everglades. Can you find three?

Female giant water bugs stick eggs onto males' backs. Spot three males and a female.

Midge larvae float in the water, eating tiny bugs. Spot seven midge larvae.

Zebra butterflies lay their eggs on passionflower leaves. Can you see four?

Deep in the jungle

The jungles of southeast Asia are as busy by night as they are by day. The left-hand page shows who comes out in the daytime and the right-hand page shows the night.

Hairy bird-eating spiders really do eat birds. They can climb trees too. Find four.

Fireflies' tummies light up, then flash on and off. Find 11.

Cockchafer beetle. Find seven.

Stay away from red centipedes. Their bites are very painful. Can you spot five?

Atlas moths are the largest moths in the world. Look hard and try to find three.

Snails slither around the jungle. Find three of each of these two kinds of snails.

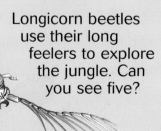

Longicorn beetles use their long feelers to explore the jungle. Can you see five?

Loepa moths have no tongues. They don't live long enough to need food. Find four.

Lantern bugs got their name because they often flutter around people's lanterns. Spot ten.

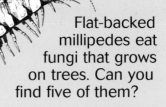

Flat-backed millipedes eat fungi that grows on trees. Can you find five of them?

These shield bugs taste horrible, so other animals don't eat them. Find seven.

Brilliant jewel beetles like lying on leaves in the warm sunshine. Find eight.

Termites march to and fro on the jungle floor. Can you spot 16 termites here?

Male cicadas make a chirping sound with a part of their tummies. Find five.

Birdwing butterflies are as big as a hand when their wings are open. Spot four.

Weaver ants make nests by sticking leaves together with spit. Can you spot 12?

Nephila spiders spin webs out of pale yellow silk. Can you spot four of them?

Minibeast safari

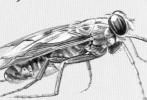

People go on expeditions, or safaris, to see the wildlife of Africa. They may not see the thousands of bugs that live there too. Spot 118 in this picture of part of South Africa.

Male rhinoceros beetles have a horn like a rhinoceros. Can you see five?

Tsetse flies drink other creatures' blood through a tube-shaped mouth. Find ten.

Swallowtail butterfly

Swallowtail caterpillar

These caterpillars wave smelly horns at enemies. Can you spot five caterpillars and three butterflies?

Potter wasps put caterpillars in their nests as food for their larvae. Find five potter wasps.

African land snails are the largest snails in the world. Can you spot four of them?

African assassin bugs work as a team, killing other insects. Find five.

Longhorn beetles chew their way into tree trunks. Find seven longhorn beetles.

African moon moths flash the eye-like markings on their wings at enemies. Spot three.

Hanging flies hang upside down from twigs with their long, skinny legs. Find eight.

Monarch butterflies eat plants that make their flesh taste horrible. Find four.

Histerid beetles like eating dung, or the bodies of dead animals. Find 21.

Ground beetles can squirt burning acid out of their bottoms. Can you spot four?

Processionary moth. Find three.

Processionary moth caterpillars wriggle along the ground in a long line. Spot ten.

Stalk-eyed flies got their name from their eyes. It's easy to see why. Find four.

A swarm of hungry locusts can eat a whole crop in hours. Spot 11 locusts.

If you disturb a praying mantis, it might wave its back wings at you. Spot six.

Insect city

Termites live in huge family groups. They build a mound of mud, spit and dung, and make a nest inside. This is what the nest looks like.

Termite mound

Only the queen termite lays eggs. She can lay over 30,000 a day. Can you find her?

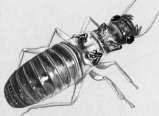

All the king termite does is mate with the queen. Can you spot him?

Worker

Eggs

Worker termites take eggs to parts of the nest called nurseries. Find four nurseries.

Worker

Larvae

The eggs hatch into pale larvae. Worker termites care for them. Find 23 larvae.

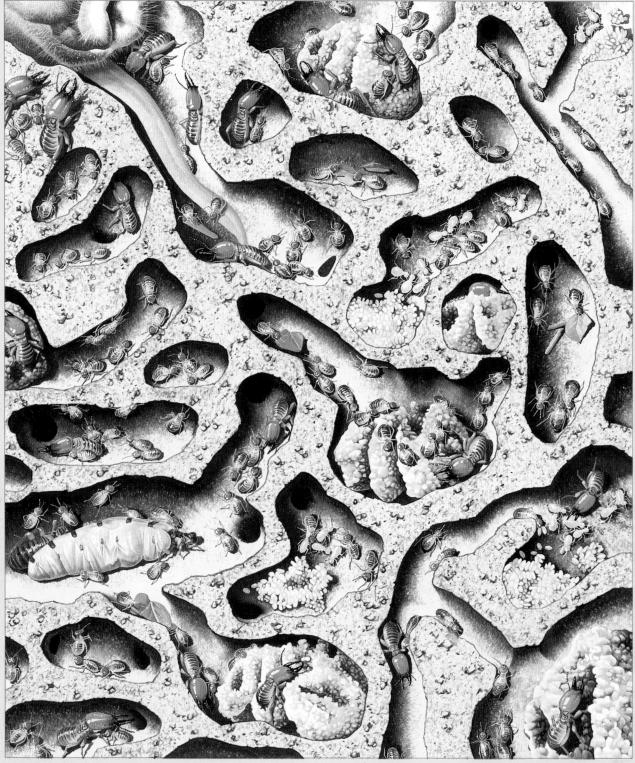

Soldier termites keep guard. They bite enemies, or squirt liquid at them. Spot 20.

Workers carry leaves into the nest in their mouths. Spot seven doing this job.

Fungus grows in "fungus gardens" in the nest. The termites eat it. Find six gardens.

Busy beehive

People keep honeybees in hives. The bees collect nectar and pollen from flowers. They eat the pollen and make the nectar into honey.

Beehive

Only the long, slim queen bee can lay eggs. Can you find her?

Drones are big male bees. They mate with the queen, then get pushed out of the hive. Find seven.

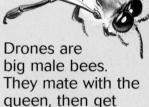
Huddling around the queen to keep her safe.

Carrying balls of pollen on their back legs.

Feeding larvae that are growing in the hive.

Worker bees do several jobs. Find three workers doing each of the things above.

Bees build little wax boxes called cells in the hive. Spot the cells being used for these things.

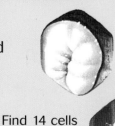
Find 17 cells with larvae in them.

Find ten cells full of pollen.

Find 14 cells full of honey.

Find 12 cells with bee eggs in them.

Worker bees sometimes spit food into another bee's mouth. Find one doing this.

Around the world

This map of the world shows the places where all the bugs in this book live.

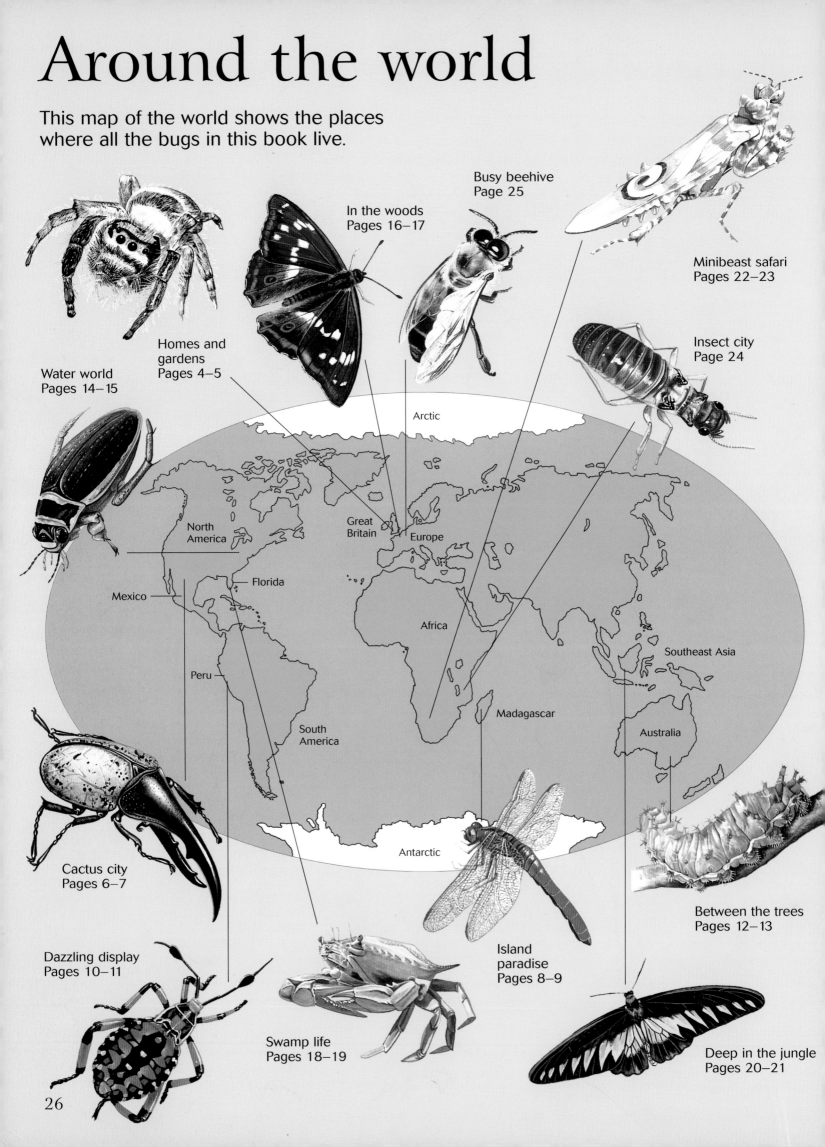

Busy beehive
Page 25

In the woods
Pages 16–17

Minibeast safari
Pages 22–23

Insect city
Page 24

Homes and gardens
Pages 4–5

Water world
Pages 14–15

Arctic

North America

Great Britain

Europe

Florida

Mexico

Africa

Southeast Asia

Peru

South America

Madagascar

Australia

Antarctic

Cactus city
Pages 6–7

Between the trees
Pages 12–13

Dazzling display
Pages 10–11

Island paradise
Pages 8–9

Swamp life
Pages 18–19

Deep in the jungle
Pages 20–21

Big bug puzzle

You've seen all these bugs earlier in the book, but can you remember anything about them? To do this puzzle, you may need to look back and find which page they're on. If you get stuck, the answers are on page 32.

1. Which of these bugs can walk on water?

2. Which bug flashes its back at enemies?

3. Which of these insects is a butterfly?

4. Which of these insects swims underwater, breathing through a tube?

5. Which of these bugs is a caterpillar?

6. Which of these bugs stores honey in its tummy?

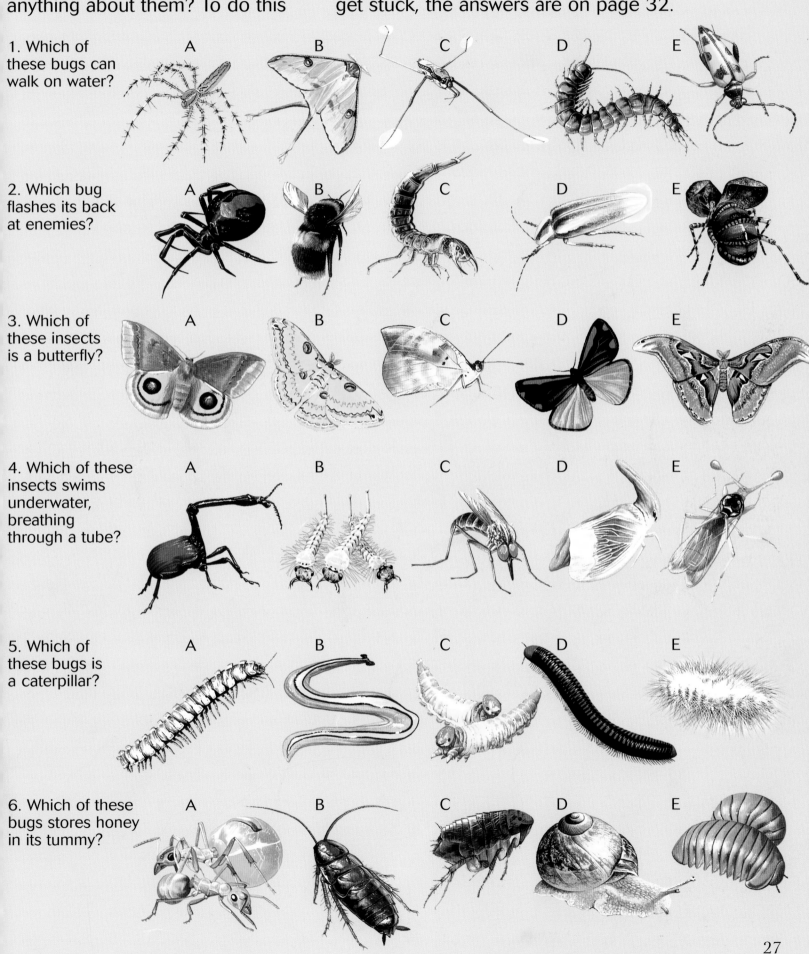

A   B   C   D   E

Homes and gardens 4–5

Male common blue butterflies 1 2 3 4
Female common blue butterflies 5 6 7 8
Honeybees 9 10 11 12 13 14 15 16 17 18
Zebra spiders 19 20 21 22 23
Centipedes 24 25 26 27 28 29
Wasps 30 31 32 33 34 35 36 37 38 39 40 41 42
Devil's coach-horses 43 44 45 46 47 48
Spittle bugs 49 50 51 52 53 54 55 56
Greenflies 57 58 59 60 61 62 63 64 65 66 67 68 69 70 71 72 73
Earwigs 74 75 76 77 78 79 80 81 82
Cockroaches 83 84 85 86 87 88 89
90 91 92 93
Lacewings 94 95 96 97 98 99 100 101 102 103 104 105 106 107
Cinnabar moths 108 109 110 111 112 113 114
Cinnabar moth caterpillars 115 116 117 118 119 120
Houseflies 121 122 123 124 125 126 127 128 129 130
Garden spiders 131 132 133 134 135 136 137 138
Fleas 139 140 141 142 143 144 145 146 147 148
Snails 149 150 151 152 153 154 155 156 157 158
Cat 159

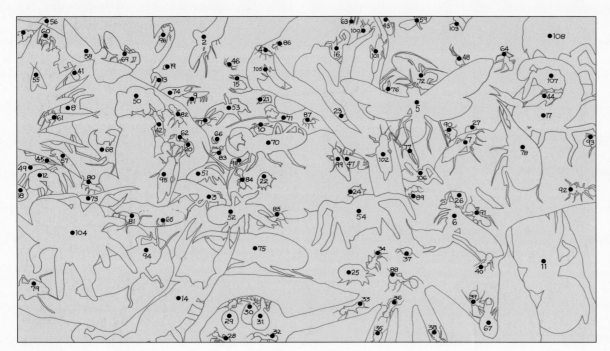

Cactus city 6–7

Tarantula hawk wasps 1 2 3 4 5 6 7
Trapdoor spiders 8 9 10 11
Scorpions 12 13 14 15 16 17
Giant red velvet mites 18 19 20 21 22 23 24 25 26 27
Honey ants 28 29 30 31 32 33 34 35 36 37 38 39 40
Blister beetles 41 42 43 44
Black widow spiders 45 46 47 48
Tarantulas 49 50 51 52 53 54
Yucca moths 55 56 57 58 59
Lynx spiders 60 61 62 63 64
Ant-lion larvae 65 66 67
Whip scorpions 68 69 70 71 72
Hercules beetles 73 74 75 76 77 78
Harvester ants 79 80 81 82 83 84 85 86 87 88 89 90 91 92 93
Painted grasshoppers 94 95 96 97 98 99 100 101 102 103
Red-kneed bird-eating spiders 104 105 106 107
Burrowing owl 108

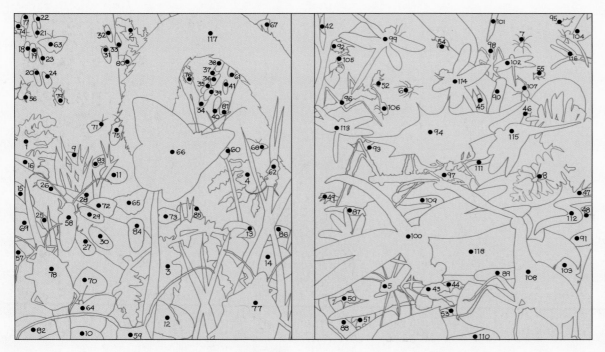

Island paradise 8–9

Praying mantis nymphs 1 2 3 4
Lynx spiders 5 6 7 8
Pill millipedes 9 10 11 12 13 14
Rosea bugs 15 16 17 18 19 20 21 22 23 24 25 26 27 28 29 30 31 32 33 34 35 36 37 38 39 40 41
Yellow hairy weevils 42 43 44 45 46 47 48
Brown hairy weevils 49 50 51 52 53 54 55
Longhorn beetles 56 57 58 59 60 61 62
Butterflies with open wings 63 64 65 66 67 68
Butterflies with shut wings 69 70 71 72 73
Shield bug adults 74 75 76 77
Shield bug nymphs 78 79 80 81
Hissing cockroaches 82 83 84 85 86
Giant millipedes 87 88 89 90 91
Thorn spiders 92 93 94 95
Stick insects 96 97 98
Emperor dragonflies 99 100 101 102 103 104
Giraffe-necked weevils 105 106 107 108
Flatworms 109 110 111 112
Red dragonflies 113 114 115 116
Ring-tailed lemur 117
Blue tree boa 118

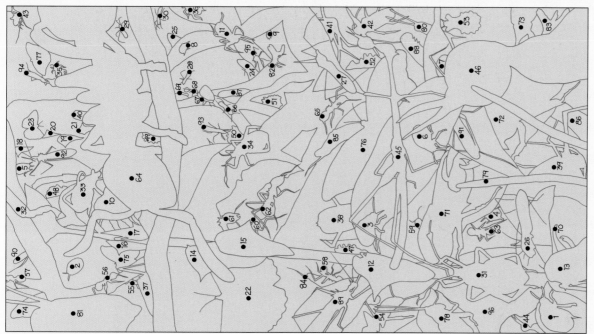

Dazzling display 10–11

Leaf beetles 1 2 3 4 5 6 7 8 9
Wandering spiders 10 11
Thornbugs 12 13 14 15 16 17 18 19 20 21
Hamadryas butterflies 22 23 24 25
Stilt bugs 26 27 28 29 30
Bright bugs 31 32 33 34 35 36
Harlequin beetles 37 38 39 40 41 42 43
Grasshoppers 44 45 46
Bark bugs 47 48 49 50 51 52 53
Leafcutter ants 54 55 56 57 58 59 60 61 62 63 64 65 66 67 68 69
Hercules beetles 70 71 72 73
Morpho butterflies 74 75 76 77

Black and yellow grasshoppers 78 79 80
Yellow, black and red grasshoppers 81 82 83
Hawk moth caterpillars 84 85 86 87 88
Assassin bugs 89 90 91 92 93 94 95
Tapir 96

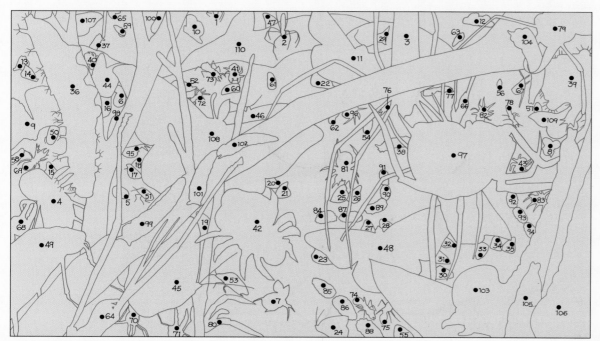

Between the trees 12–13

Net throwing spiders 1 2 3
Crickets 4 5 6 7 8
Bogong moths 9 10 11 12
Common grass yellow butterflies 13 14 15 16 17 18 19 20 21 22 23 24 25 26 27 28 29 30 31 32 33 34 35
Emperor gum moth caterpillars 36 37 38 39
Gliding spiders 40 41 42 43
Monarch butterflies 44 45 46 47 48
Shield bugs 49 50 51 52 53 54 55 56 57
Witchetty grubs 58 59 60 61 62 63
Giant stick insects 64 65 66 67
Bulldog ants 68 69 70 71 72 73 74 75 76 77 78 79

Sydney funnel-web spiders 80 81 82 83
Processionary moth caterpillars 84 85 86 87 88 89 90 91 92 93 94
Redback spiders 95 96 97
Sawfly larvae 98 99 100 101 102 103 104 105 106
Emperor gum moths 107 108 109
Bandicoot 110

Water world 14–15

Pond snails 1 2 3 4 5 6 7 8 9 10 11
Great diving beetle larvae 12 13 14 15 16
Water scorpions 17 18 19 20 21 22
Dragonfly nymphs 23 24 25 26 27
Caddisfly larvae 28 29 30 31 32
Whirligig beetles 33 34 35 36 37 38 39 40 41 42 43 44 45 46 47
Mayflies 48 49 50 51 52 53 54 55 56
Water stick insects 57 58 59 60 61
Great diving beetles 62 63 64 65 66 67 68 69 70 71
Caddisflies 72 73 74 75 76 77
Water striders 78 79 80 81 82 83 84 85

Damselflies 86 87 88 89 90 91 92
Stoneflies 93 94 95 96 97 98 99 100 101
Backswimmers 102 103 104 105 106 107
Mosquito larvae 108 109 110 111 112 113 114
Fisher spiders 115 116 117 118 119 120 121 122
Great white heron 123

29

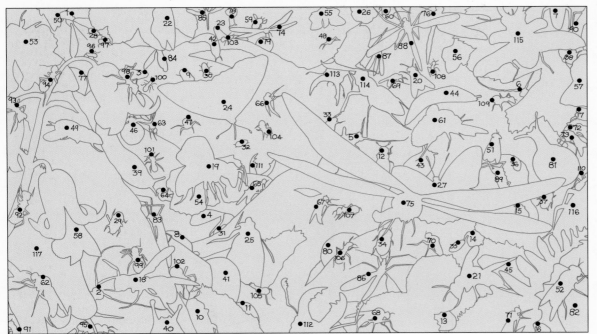

In the woods 16–17

Longhorn beetles 1
2 3 4 5 6 7
Burying beetles 8 9
10 11 12 13 14 15
16 17
Hornets 18 19 20
21
Purple emperor
butterflies 22 23 24
25 26 27
Bark beetles 28 29
30 31 32 33 34
35 36 37 38
Slugs 39 40 41 42
43 44 45
Crab spiders 46 47
48
Horseflies 49 50 51
52
Poplar hawk moths
53 54 55 56 57
Bumblebees 58 59
60 61
Empid flies 62 63
64 65 66 67 68
69 70 71 72 73
Darter dragonflies
74 75 76

Hedge snails 77 78
79 80 81 82
Crane flies 83 84 85
86 87 88 89 90
Wood ants 91 92 93
94 95 96 97 98
99 100 101 102
103 104 105 106
107 108 109 110
Stag beetles 111 112
113 114 115 116
Hedgehog 117

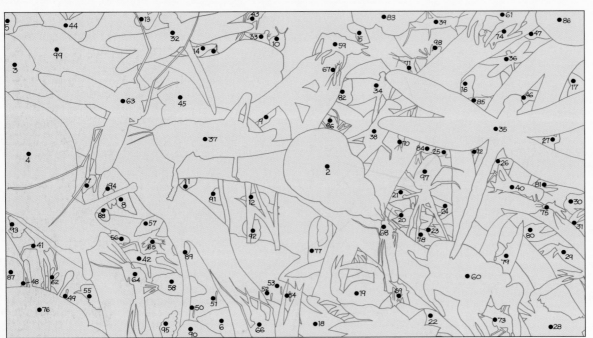

Swamp life 18–19

Tree snails 1 2 3 4
5 6 7 8 9 10 11
12
Viceroy butterflies 13
14 15 16 17
Blue land crabs 18
19 20 21 22 23
24 25 26 27 28
29 30 31
Green darner
dragonflies 32 33
34 35 36
Lubber grasshoppers
37 38 39 40
Fisher spiders 41 42
43
Zebra butterflies 44
45 46 47
Midge larvae 48 49
50 51 52 53 54
Giant water bugs 55
56 57 58
Jumping spiders 59
60 61
Mosquitoes 62 63
64 65 66 67 68
69 70 71 72 73
74 75

Fiddler crabs 76 77
78 79 80 81
Io moths 82 83 84
85 86
Apple snails 87 88
89 90 91 92
Apple snail eggs 93
94 95
Golden orb weaver
spiders 96 97 98
Alligator 99

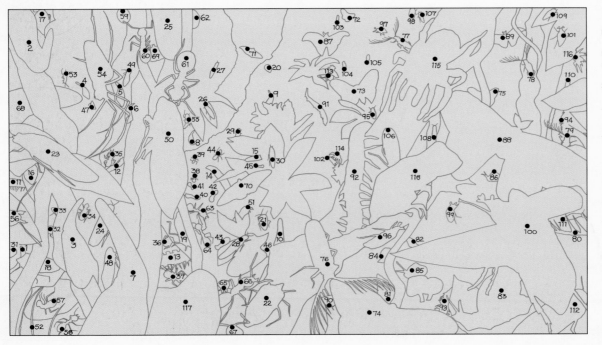

Deep in the jungle 20–21

Lantern bugs 1 2 3
4 5 6 7 8 9 10
Flat-backed
millipedes 11 12 13
14 15
Shield bugs 16 17
18 19 20 21 22
Jewel beetles 23 24
25 26 27 28 29
30
Termites 31 32 33
34 35 36 37 38
39 40 41 42 43
44 45 46
Cicadas 47 48 49
50 51
Nephila spiders 52
53 54 55
Weaver ants 56 57
58 59 60 61 62
63 64 65 66 67
Birdwing butterflies
68 69 70 71
Loepa moths 72 73
74 75
Longicorn beetles
76 77 78 79 80
Yellow snails 81 82
83

Brown snails 84 85
86
Atlas moths 87 88
89
Red centipedes 90
91 92 93 94
Cockchafer beetles
95 96 97 98 99
100 101
Fireflies 102 103
104 105 106 107
108 109 110 111
112
Hairy bird-eating
spiders 113 114 115
116
Orang-utan 117
Green tree frog 118

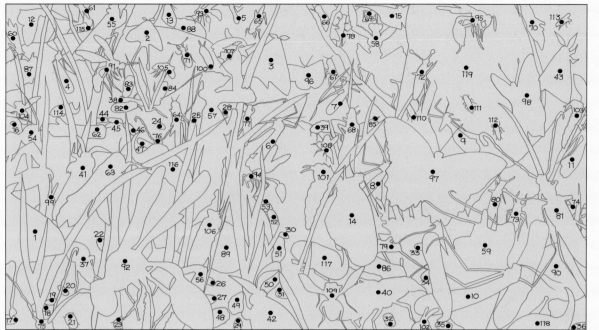

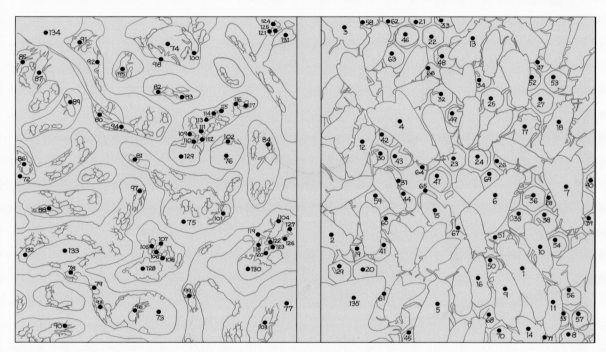

Minibeast safari 22–23

African moon moths
1 2 3
Hanging flies 4 5 6
7 8 9 10 11
Monarch butterflies
12 13 14 15
Histerid beetles 16
17 18 19 20 21
22 23 24 25 26
27 28 29 30 31
32 33 34 35 36
Ground beetles 37
38 39 40
Processionary moths
41 42 43
Processionary moth
caterpillars 44 45
46 47 48 49 50
51 52 53
Praying mantids 54
55 56 57 58 59
Locusts 60 61 62
63 64 65 66 67
68 69 70
Stalk-eyed flies 71
72 73 74
Longhorn beetles 75
76 77 78 79 80
81

African assassin
bugs 82 83 84 85
86
African land snails
87 88 89 90
Potter wasps 91 92
93 94 95
Swallowtail
butterflies 96 97 98
Swallowtail butterfly
caterpillars 99 100
101 102 103
Tsetse flies 104 105
106 107 108 109
110 111 112 113
Rhinoceros beetles
114 115 116 117
118
Kudu 119

Insect city 24

Fungus gardens 72
73 74 75 76 77
Workers carrying
leaves 78 79 80 81
82 83 84
Soldier termites 85
86 87 88 89 90
91 92 93 94 95
96 97 98 99 100
101 102 103 104

Larvae 105 106
107 108 109 110
111 112 113 114 115
116 117 118 119
120 121 122 123
124 125 126 127
Nurseries 128 129
130 131
King termite 132
Queen termite 133
Aardvark 134

Busy beehive 25

Queen bee 1
Drones 2 3 4 5 6 7
8
Workers huddling
around the queen 9
10 11
Workers carrying
balls of pollen 12 13
14
Workers feeding
larvae 15 16 17
Worker spitting 18
Pollen cells 19 20
21 22 23 24 25

26 27 28
Egg cells 29 30 31
32 33 34 35 36
37 38 39 40
Larvae cells 41 42
43 44 45 46 47
48 49 50 51 52
53 54 55 56 57
Honey cells 58 59
60 61 62 63 64
65 66 67 68 69
70 71
Mouse 135

Index

Answers to the Big bug puzzle on page 27: 1C 2E 3C 4B 5E 6A

Series editor: Felicity Brooks • Editorial assistant: Rosie Heywood • Scientific consultant: David Duthie

Cover and additional design by Stephanie Jones • Additional editing by Ben Denne and Claire Masset